Dundee: Portrait of a City

Lorn Macintyre & Peter Adamson

Spring, Camperdown Park.

First published in the United Kingdom in 2006 by Alvie Publications, 52 Buchanan Gardens, St Andrews, Fife KY16 9LX. Tel: 01334 475227.

Designed by The University of St Andrews Reprographics Unit.
Printed and bound in China by Imago.

ISBN: 0-9511800-4-5

Acknowledgements

Many people have made this book possible, not only in arranging facilities for photography, but also in reading text to check accuracy and also to share up-to-date information on research into Dundee's complex history. Thanks are due to: Lord Provost John Letford for his Foreword; Mike Arnott, Margaret Chapman and Ken Gibson, Dundee City Council; Iain Flett, City Archivist; the ever helpful staff of Dundee Central Library; Matthew Jarran and Professor Chris Whatley, University of Dundee; Professor Elaine Shemilt, Duncan of Jordanstone College of Art and Design; Lianne Bibby, Students' Association, University of Dundee; Kevin Coe, University of Abertay Dundee; Bill Downer and Eve Jamieson and Peter Royston, Dundee College; Professor Abd al-Fattah El-Awaisi, Al-Maktoum Institute; Dr Fiona Carter, Cuschieri Centre, and Brian Main, Ninewells Hospital; Maggie's Centre, Dundee; Wellcome Trust; Councillor Charles Farquhar; Peter Sinclair, Tayside Fire Brigade; Sarah Craig, Tayside Police; Fiona Sinclair, McManus Galleries and Museum; Susan Passfield, Caird Hall; High School of Dundee; Harris Academy; Morgan Academy; Ancrum Road Primary School; Grove Academy, Forthill School and Eastern Primary School, all in Broughty Ferry; Rosemary Eddy and Iain Fraser, St Pauls's Episcopal Cathedral; St Mary's Forebank; St David's High Kirk; Lochee West Church; the Steeple Church; Nicola Young, Dundee Repertory Theatre; Gill Poulter, Verdant Works; D.C. Thomson & Company Ltd; Richard Maton, National Cash Register Corporation; Dawn White Photography; Gill Christie of Cyclacel Ltd; Stewart Horne of Michelin Tyre plc; Lovat Fraser of Tayside Aviation; Dr Steve Davies of Upstate Ltd; Alan Bannerman, Phoenix Bar; John Morton, Wellgate Centre; Dr Bill Samson, Mills Observatory; Niall Cooper, *Discovery* Point; Lizzie MacGregor, Scottish Poetry Library; Alan Martin and Lynsey Thompson, Sensation; Robin Little; Duncan Stewart; Gillian Henney; Debi Briggs, figure skating head coach; Dr Andrew Jeffrey and Ian Philp, Broughty Ferry Lifeboat; Glen Pride; Gordon Low, Ottakers; Derek Robertson, Dundee United FC; Niall Scott, Dundee FC.

Quotations on the riot and fire in nineteenth century Dundee by kind permission of the *Scotsman*. The material comes from the excellent online archive of the newspaper from 1817 to 1950 accessed through scotsman.com on the web. Permission to use *Wintry Beauty* poem by William Soutar courtesy of National Library of Scotland, Edinburgh. Photographs of the Cathedral Church of St Paul taken by kind permission of the Provost and Vestry. Simon Reekie painting, and other paintings and artefacts photographed by kind permission of McManus Galleries and Museum.

To all others, too numerous to mention, grateful thanks.

A Tayside Aviation Grob plane approaches the Tay Railway Bridge. Dundee now has a thriving airport.

Foreword

Dundee, Scotland's 4th city created in the 12th century, situated on the north side of the most beautiful river in Scotland beckons our visitors with promises and glimpses of our rich heritage past, present and future.

Peter Adamson's view through the eye of his well known and respected camera opens up an Aladdin's cave of riches and takes us on an interesting journey of Discovery.

This book is the latest example of the highly successful collaboration between Lorn Macintyre and Peter Adamson. Dr Lorn Macintyre, highly acclaimed Scottish writer, directs the reader's attention through picture to text with fascinating comment on present day Dundee.

It tells us of a city that has rediscovered itself through invention and innovation, a city that boasts two Universities of academic excellence, medical research, new technologies, biotechnology and a city renowned for its renaissance in arts and culture.

Redevelopment has invaded our medieval landscape, but not eradicated it and our rich history is still evident. Gardyne's Land, the Auld Steeple, HM Frigate Unicorn, and RRS Discovery are typical examples and all await our waterfront development that will embrace our beautiful river and indeed will be our Jewel in the Crown.

Enjoy your trip throughout our city courtesy of Lorn's distinguished text and Peter's magnificent photography, which I am sure will be a lasting experience.

John Letford
Lord Provost of Dundee

Introduction

When does the history of Dundee begin – with a gnawed porpoise bone left by one of the early settlers round the Tay estuary, or with a charter ponderous with seals? In one version of the story, Dundee got its name when, between 1178 and 1182, William the Lion granted lands on Tayside to his brother David, Earl of Huntington, and, it is claimed, David showed his thanks for his delivery from the infidel in a Crusade by founding a church dedicated to the Blessed Virgin Mary, one of Dundee's patron saints. The other is St Clement, patron saint of mariners, an uncommon duality pointing to a possible Viking link, as they were fond of this combination as well.

Dundee was made a burgh in the early 1190s. Its coat of arms has the motto *Dei Donum* (Gift of God), believed to be a pun on the Latin place name *Taodunum* which is used for Dundee in Blaeu's *Atlas*. Other derivations for the name have been put forward, such as *dun Deagh* (Gaelic: fortress of Daigh), perhaps after some forgotten warrior called Daig, possibly a personal name derived from *daig* (fire).

The city became embroiled in the Scottish Wars of Independence, and was occupied by the English in 1291. Five years later Edward the First destroyed St Mary's Church, and so God's Gift became the site of the Devil's work.

But what do the hypotheses of historians matter about the origin of names when Dundonians are convinced that theirs is the finest city in Scotland, even though some places where they are now walking were once under water? The shoreline of Dundee used to run in front of the Seagate and the bottom of Castle Street. Dundee's docks were constructed on reclaimed land, and later filled in, so that people are strolling on what was the Tay. Recent excavations for the foundations for some of Dundee's new and restored properties have uncovered underground arched vaults – including one containing mercury, not from a centuries-old shipment, but more recent industrial contamination.

It has been noted that Dundee is laid out to the design of a Baltic port, because of its importance in international trade. The wynds which led down towards the sea were curved to deflect the bitter winds, though the merchants had well-lined cloaks in contrast to the thin garments of the poor, the rags of beggars. Dundee's infant mortality rate was the highest in Scotland in the overcrowded slums round the mills. The jails were full, juveniles sharing cells with adults. Cholera lurked round every corner, and water from a tap was an unheard-of luxury.

The saintly Mary Lily Walker of the Dundee Social Union and that visionary town planner James Thomson helped to transform the city, fighting for social equality and clearing the slums. The poet Hugh MacDiarmid condemned Dundee in 1934 as a 'grim monument to man's inhumanity to man.' No writer could say this of present-day Dundee. Prosperous and elegant, it can compete with any city in Scotland and beyond.

Lorn Macintyre
March 2006

Spanning the Tay

The Christmas parcels had been opened, and there was a new year to look forward to. W.H. Benyon, photographer, Cheltenham, was one of the passengers on the night of 28 December 1879 as the train approached the Tay Bridge in the ferocious storm. His decision to go to Dundee was a last-minute one, after settling with a colleague as to who should cover the northern district.

Hailed as one of the engineering wonders of its time, the Tay railway bridge, opened in the summer of 1879, was of advanced lattice-grid design, combining cast and wrought iron, a state-of-the-art method for that age of confidence. Thomas Bouch, who constructed the bridge, was a noted railway engineer, and received a knighthood for spanning the Tay estuary.

As the carriage began to topple off the bridge that festive season night in 1879 Benyon cast off his ulster coat, presumably to give him a better chance of reaching the shore once the train hit the Tay. The *Scotsman* for 9 February 1880 announced the recovery of the photographer's body at Newport. He had £18 on his person, and 'two massive gold rings were also taken off his fingers, one a diamond ring, and the other a gold buckle ring, both of great value.' Did he have a premonition of disaster, because his life was insured for £1000 with the Accidental Assurance Company? The flashily dressed photographer went home in a 'richly ornamented' coffin of polished oak.

Seventy five lives had been lost, including the son-in-law of Sir Thomas Bouch. The cylindrical cast iron columns supporting the thirteen longest spans of the bridge were found to be of poor quality, and no allowance had been made for wind load. Bouch died broken-hearted within a year of the tragedy, and the Victorian poet William Topaz McGonagall commemorated this event in doggerel.

As you cross the bridge in one of the modern trains you can see the pillars of the doomed span in the swirling waters below.

A happier tale of the Tay bridge disaster: the small robe of fine white lawn with panels of Indian embroidery which had been in a parcel on the fatal train was washed up without its wrapping at Broughty Ferry and identified by the indelible inscription on the linen: 'To A. Lorimer from A.D. F[errier].' Purchased as a gift in Calcutta, the robe was duly delivered to Mr and Mrs Adolphus Lorimer, who were expecting their first child. The gift yielded up by the sea was worn for the christenings of the Lorimers' seven children, and, to date, by five generations of the family, including Glen Pride the architect, his daughters and grand-children.

The Tay road bridge, which lies to the east of the Tay rail bridge and was designed by William Fairhurst, is a concrete multispanned toll bridge. With its 1.4 miles (2250 m) span, it is one of the longest bridges in Europe. West Graving Dock, King William Dock and Earl Grey dock were infilled as part of the construction. The late Queen Elizabeth the Queen Mother opened the bridge on 18 August 1966. Though high winds sometimes disrupt its traffic, the road bridge is an essential artery of Dundee, as is the neighbouring railway bridge.

The crossing into Fife at dusk shows the elegance of the road bridge.

The Tay rail bridge, crossing of tragedy.

From Great Tay of the Waves

O that yon river micht nae mair

Rin through the channels o' my sleep;

My bluid has felt its tides owre sair,

Its waves hae drooned my dreams owre deep.

Lewis Spence (1874-1955)

The jute phenomenon

A stranger standing at the gates of the Cox brothers' 30 acre Camperdown Works at Lochee in the Victorian era would have been bowled over by the surge at the end of the shift. Children who have spent the day crawling under dangerous machines rush to meet their friends who have been at school. Weary looking women, their hands tainted by the whale oil used to soften the jute fibres, clatter home in their clogs to feed families. Female weavers in rakish hats shout insults as they light cigarettes and decide on the evening's entertainment. Mr Cox has left by a separate exit to be conveyed home to his mansion by his own coachman. His workforce of 6000 supports a princely lifestyle. He can afford to be generous, to throw pennies to street urchins. With over 43,000 souls employed in the mills in and around Dundee, profits are enormous.

The mills were modern buildings, with up-to-date machinery, and some places had medical staff and teachers for child workers. Though the wages were not generous, the mill owners provided public parks and buildings for the recreation and enlightenment of their workers, in an age when philanthropy was approached with religious zeal.

As Professor Christopher Whatley of Scottish History at the University of Dundee has said: 'what came back to haunt the Dundee jute industry was that the region's engineering firms and its mill managers and skilled mechanics played key parts in establishing the works of its rivals in Calcutta.'

A Second World War brought big orders for sandbags, but afterwards female workers were lured away to the new American firms which opened up on the city's fringes. The partitioning of the Indian subcontinent into the independent states of India and Pakistan restricted British supplies of both raw jute and finished jute goods. In 1946 a Board of Trade committee recommended the protection of the Dundee mills from the competition from Calcutta. Re-equipment and reorganization seemed the best hopes for survival, and between 1945 and 1951 an estimated £4 million was laid out. Prices of imported jute goods were adjusted through Control to protect Dundee's producers from India's industrious mills. The mills that were left had to adapt – not all successfully – to more modern fibres.

What was a day in the life of a worker in a mill like? Visit the Verdant Works for an unforgettable hands-on experience, whatever your age. Absorb the sights and smells of the machine room, sense the earth tremble as the original machines roar into life and listen to the workers' hopes, fears and dreams when the female weavers waved their gloved hands from the tops of homeward-bound omnibuses as though they were royalty.

It looks as if this handsome worker is handling golden fleeces. Actually he's engaged in the process of batching, mixing bales of jute of different qualities and colours to suit a customer's requirements. He's separating and twisting the jute by hand into heads or bundles, preparatory to the fibres being softened and sprayed with an emulsion, or mixture of oil and water, which will make the manufacturing process easier. Watch him in the Verdant Works.

Is the top-hatted gent leaning on the cane one of the Verdant Mill's shareholders, ensuring that the typist understands her new-fangled machine? Or is he perhaps looking over her shoulder to see rising production figures – and hence profits – though it's dubious if he'll live to enjoy them?

Camperdown Works was recognized as the finest example of a Victorian mill building in Britain, which is why Dundee City Council was determined to save it from decay and vandalism. James F Stephen Architects converted the building into 74 high quality flatted dwellings, retaining the clock tower and cast iron cupola as a feature. The sympathetic restoration (total cost, around £5 million) included a complete new roof, and new windows to embody the spirit of the mill. To the right of the tower is the Stack Leisure Park, for flat dwellers who feel energetic.

The enduring monument to the dominance of the mill in Dundee, the 282 foot high patterned brick chimney of Cox's Stack was the landmark of the 30 acre Camperdown Works, designed by G.A. Cox between 1861-68. The stack, added by James Maclaren in 1865-66, was meant to show that Camperdown and Cox were supreme in a city which had several ornate mills with pediments and cupolas.

Councillor Charles Farquhar, OBE, aka 'Mr Lochee', with the clock tower of Camperdown Works where his mother started her shift in the dawn, and gave her son the sense of dedication and determination to serve the city of Dundee for over forty years, including holding the highest office of Provost.

Two Dundee ships

As the heels of visitors sound on the deck of *Discovery* as it lies in its smart berth on Dundee's waterfront, think of Captain Robert Scott pacing that same deck as the vessel lies imprisoned in ice in McMurdo Sound in June 1902, darkness 24 hours a day because the sun cannot be seen from within the Antarctic Circle. The Captain and his crew are wondering if they will see their homes again.

Come the spring (September), the weather improved and Scott, Dr Wilson and Ernest Shackleton set off south with dog sledges across the Ross Sea ice shelf towards the Pole. Scott travelled slightly further than 82 degrees south, much further than anyone before. They were reduced to man-hauling because the dogs died due to a poor diet. The dog food, made of dried fish, had few nutrients and had probably gone bad. Scott was squeamish about killing and eating the dogs, and they didn't know the sacrifice could have abated the scurvy that had incapacitated Shackleton.

Axes bounce off the endless white expanse of ice in which *Discovery* is trapped, so they use explosives to blast their way back to life. Scott wrote: 'Thus it was that after she had afforded us shelter and comfort for two full years, and after we had borne a heavy anxiety on her behalf, our good ship was spared to take us homeward. On 16 February 1904, the Discovery came to her own again – the right to ride the high seas.' She arrived back in England that September to a rapturous welcome.

Discovery brought them home because it was built in Dundee. The vessel is part of the award-winning Discovery Point Antarctic Museum, an essential embarkation point for a lesson in courage and endurance.

The frigate *Unicorn* echoes with the shouts of an instructor, the vibrations of the timbers as members of the Royal Naval Reserve drill. Many of them would be lost in the great sea battles of two world wars. *Unicorn* is the oldest British-built ship still afloat, having been launched in 1824 and after years as a powder-hulk, was brought to the Earl Grey Dock in Dundee in 1873 as a drill ship, and almost scrapped when it became known that the Dock was to be filled in. However, she was reprieved and moved to Victoria Dock in 1962.

The ship is maintained by the Unicorn Preservation Society and is now part of an exhibit within City Quay, the regeneration project centred on the Victoria Dock. If you want to sample life in the Royal Navy in the glorious (but taxing) era of sail, step on board – and be sure to salute.

The golden horn of HMS *Unicorn's* figurehead. The original effigy of the mythical beast was wooden, but has now been replaced by a glass fibre moulding which is much more weatherproof.

Safe from the breaker's yard, HMS *Unicorn* in its smart dock.

A gun on board HMS *Unicorn*, never tried in battle.

RRS *Discovery,* like a toy boat in its berth.

The swivel seats in RRS *Discovery*, perhaps to save spillage of drinks at a loyal toast. As a further indulgence, the seats were also reversible, leather for a cold climate, basket-weave for the Tropics.

Dundee's Architecture

Now that the town's barriers have been trampled down, one of General Monck's troops pursues a Dundonian down one of the town's wynds, and when the fugitive takes refuge in one of the timber buildings, it's easier to torch it than follow him into the hovel. Flames and cannon damaged and destroyed many of the medieval buildings of the town in September 1651. Yet only seventy or so years later, when the spy Daniel Defoe visited Dundee, he reported: 'It is exceedingly populous, full of stately houses, and large handsome streets…'

But what of the ordinary worker? In the nineteenth century the trunks of Irish emigrants were unloaded from the ships that had taken them from a land of famine and prejudice. In the slums they shared with rodents they died from typhus and tainted water, and some, no doubt, from a sense of hopelessness. The townhouse gaol became as overcrowded as the houses, because poverty breeds petty crime and domestic violence.

As families crowded into rooms industrial dynasties like the Baxters and Coxs who had made fortunes were commissioning distinguished architects to build them massive mansion houses. But public buildings such as David Bryce's Royal Exchange, designed in imitation of a Flemish cloth hall, and Sir George Gilbert Scott's Albert Institute (built with private capital) were also being erected.

It was fortuitous for Dundee that James Thomson was made City Architect in 1904 and City Engineer in 1906. A visionary influenced by Patrick Geddes (who has been hailed as the 'father of modern town planning'), and by the work of the Social Union, James Thomson drew up plans for the transformation of Dundee.

Improvement is often a precarious balance between the old and the new, and Thomson had to take into account the advent of the motor car. Old buildings had to be sacrificed to widen streets. But Thomson did modernize the housing stock by building the ground-breaking Logie housing scheme after the First World War. Claimed to be the first council housing estate in Scotland, Logie's wide streets lined with trees represented the nearest to heaven for those who could afford to move out of crowded city housing.

Other housing estates followed in the 1930s, and even sun balconies were provided for workers who had spent their days in the gloom of a factory. After the Second World War, international companies such as Timex moved into factories built along the Kingsway, with peripheral housing schemes needed for the workers.

Today Dundee is a conglomeration of styles that never fails to surprise, and often to delight. Behind a plastic façade in the city centre, an original building, and here, a wrought iron gate leading to a wynd of restored houses, a moment to pause and to hear again a trooper's heels in hot pursuit.

Mindful of the money he had made in his mill, and with a genuine care for the citizens of Dundee, the jute baron Sir James Caird donated £100,000 towards a new city hall and concert hall for Dundee just before the First World War was to relegate such philanthropy to history. Sir James specified that James Thomson, the city's architect, was to design the building. Mrs Marryat, Sir James's sister, provided the £75,000 to complete the hall and lounge, after the death of her brother in 1916, and following difficulties with materials and labour during the war. The lounge became the Marryat Hall in her memory. The main hall could seat over 3,000, with room on the platform for a 75 piece orchestra, plus a 300 strong choir.

Is the seagull about to make a deposit on the Clydesdale Bank building on the High Street? Designed by William Spence (1876), its rich Renaissance details don't seem out of place in a city of merchant princes.

As an example of how Dundee is changing literally overnight, this walkway between Tayside House and the railway station was demolished in mid August 2005 over two nights, with minimum disruption to the public.

Happy Hillock Road in Mid Craigie sounds like a name out of a D.C. Thomson comic, and is certainly colourful.

From inside St Paul's Cathedral,
a perspective on the modern
city, but with evocative names
retained for the tower blocks:
Bonnethill Court and
Butterburn Court.

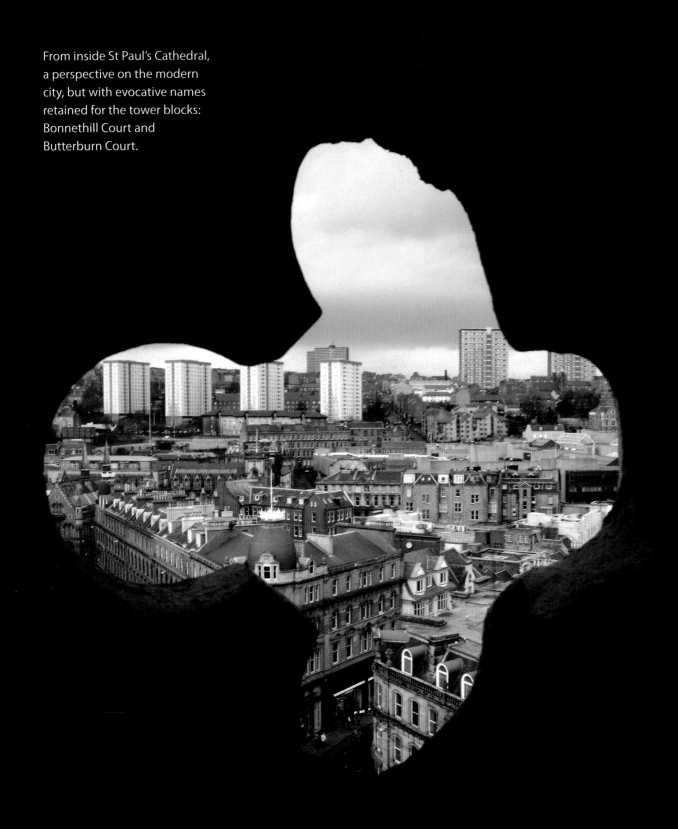

The photographer must have had friends in high places to be allowed to climb the tower of St Paul's Cathedral to take this view of the High Street, whose buildings were once the pride of old Dundee. Locate the plaque on the wall that leads you through Gray's Close to Gardyne's Land, the oldest residential building in Dundee. The first recorded owner of the building in 1560 was John Gardyne who presumably gave it its name. Gardyne's Land and adjacent buildings on the High Street are being restored by Dundee City Council in association with the Tayside Building Preservation Trust, with, hopefully, beds for backpackers where merchants once slept in four posters under painted ceilings.

Erected in 1586, the Mercat Cross was the centre of mercantile life in Dundee. But it became a victim of the city's prosperity in 1777, when it had to be removed from the west end of High Street because it was obstructing horse-drawn traffic. The unicorn on top is a modern reproduction in resin-bronze by Scott Sutherland RSA, raised on John Mylne's original carved shaft.

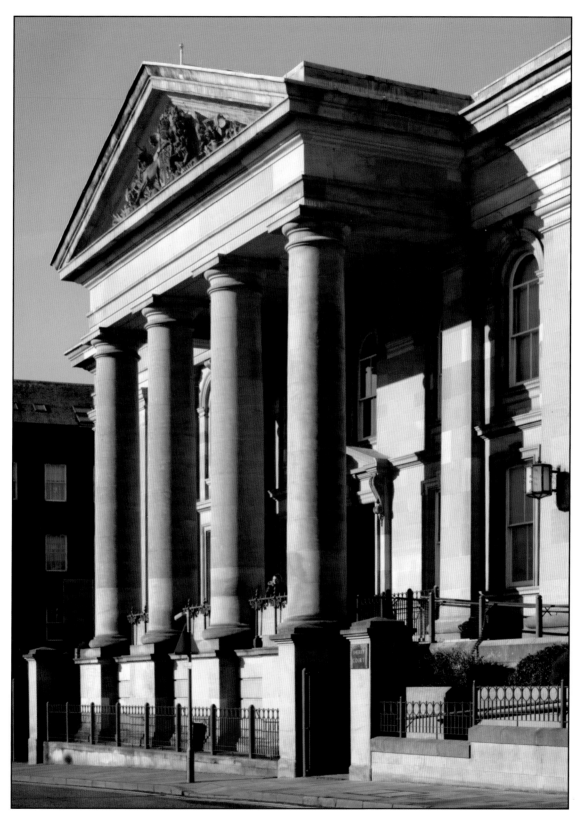

How many miscreants have passed under the portico of the Sheriff Court Building in West Bell Street, designed by George Angus in 1833, with additions by William Scott in 1863?

Top left: Fountains soothe in the city centre. The four standing forms in the water are inscribed with poems and are the imaginative work of Lizzanne Kempsell as part of Dundee Public Art Programme.

Top right: From D.C. Thomson's Meadowside building, a view of the Howff, donated to the burgh by Queen Mary in 1564 as a burial ground. The Howff took its name (meeting place) from the macabre fact that the Dundee Incorporated Trades met among the funerary monuments to conduct business. Today it is a place of peace and reflection in a busy city.

Left: D.C. Thomson's headquarters in Meadowside was designed in 1902 by Niven and Wigglesworth of London. Visiting Americans would have seen aspects of style from the New World, because Wigglesworth had visited the William Randolph Hearst empire in America. However, his colleague, David Barclay Niven from Angus, kept any excesses in check. As the architectural historians Professor Charles McKean and David Walker have commented in their indispensable *Illustrated Introduction* to Dundee: 'The result is a confident, tall, red stone, steel-framed building with engaging sculptural details by Albert Hodge.'

On the extinct volcano of the Law,
Dundee's poignant landmark, the massive
memorial to the fallen in two world wars.

The Murraygate from the Wellgate Centre on a sunny day. Here, in the eighteenth century the gentry strutted in the winter months, with their canes and snuffboxes, 'in sullen hauteur.' Dundee folk are much friendlier now, and will point out to you tramlines that used to take them to their work, and ornamental lamp standards under which they courted after the dancing.

Shore Street, a perilous crossing.

Many pupils from as far afield as St Andrews rely on buses to take them to and from the High School of Dundee.

The gentleman hasn't buckled the railings by leaning on them outside the Overgate.

Ward Road has elegant buildings and energetic shoppers.

The gentleman in the top hat standing at the foot of Blackness Avenue on the morning of Monday 12 August 1839 takes his gold hunter from his waistcoat pocket to check the time. It is precisely 9.45, and into sight comes Mr Cruickshank's horse-drawn omnibus. The gentleman in the top hat, having done his business for the day, is waiting at 'a quarter before four in the afternoon' at St Andrews Street for the omnibus to take him home, having helped to inaugurate Dundee's first bus service, fare, three old pence. The photograph was taken in Lochee.

Commissioned by Dundee Public Art Programme, this attractive erection in the Marketgait is in the form of a water derrick because the Scourie burn runs nearby in a culvert. The sculpture was a collaboration between Chris Biddlecombe and Chris Kelly who both took degrees in Public Art at Duncan of Jordanstone College of Art and Design.

This stylish pyramid at Hawkhill looks as if it might be marking the resting place of a Dundee hero. Actually it was built over a public convenience in the 1980s which is now closed, leaving Stan Bonnar's monument high and dry, so to speak.

The city from the Steeple Church.

In the early nineteenth century the Grahams of Fintry sold their seat, Mains Castle (or Fintry), above the burn in the Dichty valley in Caird Park, but left behind a Renaissance stone panel with a motto in Latin, giving thanks for their sojourn, and perhaps also making a plea for the building's survival: *grateful for country, for friends, and for posterity.* After recent impressive restoration, the castle with its six storey tower and grand staircase has become a restaurant and function venue.

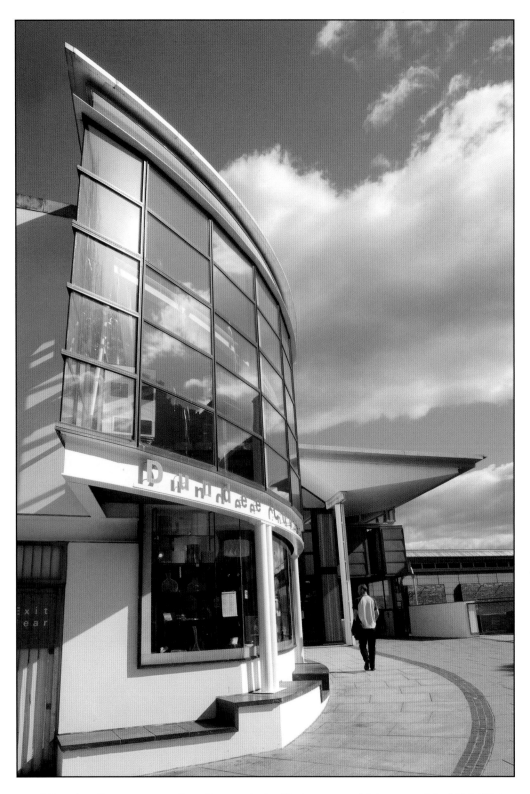

The stylish curve of Dundee Contemporary Arts Centre on the Nethergate, which opened in 1999. With nearly a million visitors to date, it brings quality international shows to the city as well as encouraging local talent and activities. There are five floors of galleries, a print centre, educational facilities, the University of Dundee visual research centre and a shop. In the Jute Café Bar, ponder the city's artistic vibrancy over a coffee.

A row of terrace houses on Hawkhill withstands the encroachments of modernism in the form of the Wellcome Trust building.

The elegant staircase in the Wellcome Trust building.

The stained glass window which spans three floors of the Wellcome Trust building was created by Julian Stocks and is entitled 'Uses of Disorder.'

Science is hands-on fun at Sensation in Greenmarket, where dozens of specially designed interactive exhibits demonstrate how vital sight, sound, touch, smell and taste are to us as we move about a busier and more complicated world.

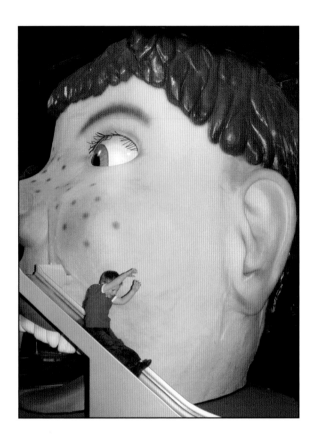

If the two children had met these creatures when they roamed the earth, they wouldn't be lingering. The large bird-like one is Gastornis, and the smaller mammal Leptictidium, about to become the bigger one's lunch. The creatures were part of *Walking with Beasts,* a BBC touring exhibition which came to Sensation in Greenmarket.

The Steeple Church, one of Dundee's best known and loved landmarks, has had a turbulent and complicated history. Built as St Mary's Church at the close of the twelfth century by David Earl of Huntingdon, brother to King William the Lion of Scotland, in gratitude for the Earl's safe return from a Crusade, the church was sacked a century later by Edward 1 of England, but rebuilt. Damaged by strife and conflagration down the centuries, only the Tower and St Clement's were left standing. Two churches were rebuilt on to the remaining structure – the South Church in a shorter transept, and St. Mary's beyond it at the east end. In time, South Church was renamed St Paul's. In 1989 the Steeple Church celebrated its bi-centenary with the creation of the Welcoming Hall within the church, and has a vibrant growing congregation which strives to serve the community in which it is situated.

A couple take their vows at the altar of St Mary's Forebank Roman Catholic church, its soaring romanesque interior (1850) the impressive work of George Mathewson.

The magnificent interior of St Paul's Episcopal Cathedral, Sir George Gilbert Scott's lofty creation on a restricted site.

This beautiful brass marks the last resting place in St Paul's of Alexander Penrose Forbes, Bishop of Brechin (1847-75), who was responsible for building the Cathedral. In the sanctuary there is also a memorial to this man revered for his profound spirituality and social commitment in nineteenth century Dundee.

St David's High Kirk, Kinghorne Road, with the war memorial on the Law in the background.

Lochee West Church, with seating for 1000, was designed by James MacLaren and opened for worship on 24 September 1871, when the collection was £1,009.

Self-portrait of a famous Dundonian

My Dear Readers of this autobiography, which I am the author of, I beg leave to inform you that I was born in Edinburgh. My parents were born in Ireland, and my father was a handloom weaver, and he learned me the handloom weaving while in Dundee, and I followed it for many years, until it began to fail owing to machinery doing the weaving instead of the handloom. So much so as I couldn't make a living from it. But I may say Dame Fortune has been very kind to me by endowing me with the genius of poetry. I remember how I felt when I received the spirit of poetry. It was in the year of 1877, and in the month of June, when trees and flowers were in full bloom. Well, it being the holiday week in Dundee, I was sitting in my back room in Paton's Lane, Dundee, lamenting to myself because I couldn't get to the Highlands on holiday to see the beautiful scenery, when all of a sudden my body got inflamed, and instantly I was seized with a strong desire to write poetry, so strong, in fact, that in imagination I thought I heard a voice crying in my ears

"WRITE! WRITE"

I wondered what could be the matter with me, and I began to walk backwards and forwards in a great fit of excitement, saying to myself – "I know nothing about poetry." But still the voice kept ringing in my ears – "Write, write," until at last, being overcome with a desire to write poetry, I found paper, pen, and ink, and in a state of frenzy, sat me down to think what would be my first subject for a poem. All at once I thought of the late Rev. George Gilfillan, and composed a poem of four stanzas in his praise as a preacher, and orator, and poet. Then I sent it to the "Weekly News" for publication, not sending my name with it, only my initials – W. McG., Dundee. It was published, along with a short comment by the editor in its praise, as follows:- " W. McG., Dundee, has sent us a poem in praise of the Rev. George Gilfillan, and he sung his praises truly and well, but he modestly seeks to hide his light under a bushel" so when I read the poem in the "Weekly News" I was highly pleased no doubt to see such a favourable comment regarding it. Then my next poem, or second, was the *"Railway Bridge of the Silvery Tay"*, which caused a great sensation in Dundee and far away. In fact, gentle readers, it was the only poem that made me famous universally.

W. McG.: William McGonagall

Minnie the Minx threatens passers-by in the city centre. The brilliant creation of Leo Baxendale at the suggestion of *Beano* editor George Moonie, Minnie made her first appearance in the comic in time for Christmas 1953. A first cousin to Dennis the Menace, Minnie's speciality is beating up boys – often dozens at a time.

He isn't as fierce as he was when he first joined Dennis the Menace in the *Beano* in 1968. But Gnasher has mellowed over the years, and his many young fans find him cuddly despite the display of terrifying teeth.

He is one of Dundee's most loved sons, recognizable the world over. Desperate Dan struts his stuff in City Square, though his gut from his intake of cow pie makes him look in imminent danger of a heart attack.

The colourful Lord Provost's Youth Parade, involving over 800 youngsters, passes the Steeple Church as it winds its way through the city centre. Part of the Dundee Youth Festival, it is hoped that the Youth Parade will become an annual event.

Malcolm Archibald was the winner of the Dundee Book Prize for 2005 in competition with 200 other contestants. Malcolm received the £6000 cash prize for his first novel, entitled *Whales for the Wizard,* a fast-paced adventure story set around the whaling industry in Dundee in the 1860s.

Back in his home city, Allan Neave, Artistic Director of the Dundee International Guitar Festival and one of the foremost classical guitarists of his time, has a contemplative rest at Dundee Contemporary Arts Centre.

The telescope may be the correct length, but the legs of Admiral Adam Duncan on his statue outside St Paul's Cathedral have been deemed to be too short. The son of a Dundee Lord Provost, he joined the navy at the age of 14, and is famous for his victory over the Dutch at Camperdown in 1797. Part of his family estates now forms Camperdown Park in Dundee.

Appropriate to Burns' Monument in Dundee

While Genius, needy wretch, was yet alive,

No generous patron would a dinner give;

See him, when starved to death and turned to dust,

Presented with a monumental bust.

The poet's fate is here in emblem shown –

He asked for bread and he received a stone.

Epitaph for Samuel Butler,
adapted by Archibald Paul.

For the last time, before being absorbed into the Royal Regiment of Scotland, the Black Watch marches through the city with bayonets fixed, drums beating and colours flying, an entitlement that dates back to 1954, when it was granted the freedom of Dundee. Many sons of Dundee have fought and fallen with the regiment in wars down the centuries.

The Comin' o' the Spring

There's no a muir in my ain land but's fu' o' sang the day,

Wi' the whaup, and the gowden plover, and the lintie upon the brae.

The birk in the glen is springin', the rowan-tree in the shaw,

And every burn is rinnin' wild wi' the meltin' o' the snaw.

The wee white clouds in the blue lift are hurryin' light and free,

Their shadows fleein' on the hills, where I, too, fain wad be;

The wind frae the west is blawin, and wi' it seems to bear

The scent o' the thyme and gowan thro' a' the caller air.

The herd doon the hillside's linkin'. O licht his heart may be

Whose step is on the heather, his glance ower muir and lea!

On the Moss are the wild ducks gatherin', whar the pules like diamonds lie,

And far up soar the wild geese, wi' weird unyirdly cry.

In mony a neuk the primrose lies hid frae stranger een,

An' the broom on the knowes is wavin' wi' its cludin' o' gowd and green;

Ower the first green springs o' heather the muir-fowl faulds his wing,

And there's nought but joy in my ain land at the comin' o' the Spring!

Lady John Scott (1810-1900)

Snowdrops at Camperdown House, William Burn's mansion for the son and heir of Admiral Duncan, Viscount Camperdown. The stately home and policies have been described as among Dundee's glories.

Daffodils wander in Dudhope Park.

They have not come down from the hills of Angus to forage in Dundee Technology Park, but are the lifelike (and award-winning) creation in cold cast resin of David Annand.

Perhaps you were on the last train that rattled through this tunnel 40 or so years ago, and threw your apple core out of a window. If so it has grown into a laden tree in the Miley Road Urban Wildlife Reserve in the centre of Dundee, developed by the Scottish Wildlife Trust, where creatures from the surrounding countryside and city gardens have found a haven. As you walk, watch the hovering kestrel, or glimpse a red squirrel flowing along a branch.

The seat of the Scrimgeours, Hereditary Constables of Dundee, Dudhope Castle has had a chequered history. Dating from 1580 onwards, the baronial castle passed to John Graham of Claverhouse, the Jacobite hero immortalized as 'Bonnie Dundee,' and then to the Duke of Douglas. Daniel Defoe judged it 'a noble and ancient pile.' In 1792 a scheme to establish a woollen factory in the building was abandoned. From 1796 to 1897 the castle was used as barracks, accommodating several hundred soldiers, and thereafter the estate became a public park. Today Dudhope, with its ornamental gardens and lush green lawns, has a new lease of life as the Dundee Business School of the University of Abertay Dundee.

Dundee schools

Education came early to Dundee, with its Grammar School (precursor of the present High School) mentioned in documents circa 1224, with the abbey of Lindores across the Tay having the right to appoint the master. There must have been many boys whose smarting posteriors reminded them of Latin declensions. Their sisters had to sit at home, learning what they could in the family circle.

However, throughout the centuries, education has been a privilege, not a right, though there were those who saw it as a moral corrective. The 'ragged' school arose out of Victorian concern that the poor would grow up without education, and fall into dissolute habits. In Dundee the managers of the 'ragged' schools approached the employers of drunken parents for some of their wages to be paid direct to the schools to help educate the children.

When the Burgh School Board was created in 1873, it found itself with no schools to administer, since the Grammar School, the Academy and the English School had been brought together under one roof as Dundee Public Seminaries (now the High School) which were administered by directors. The School Board was about to take over the financially embarrassed Seminaries, when ex Baillie William Harris offered £10,000 so that the Board could build its own school for advanced teaching.

Naturally, the new school, opened in 1885, was called Harris Academy. Dundonian children were not slothful school goers, because on the opening day 1,035 pupils enrolled, and the accommodation soon proved insufficient. More desks were needed, but where in the city?

John Morgan, a Dundonian who had prospered in India, left his fortune for the benefit of his native city, but his will was disputed in the courts. The city won the case, and the Morgan Hospital, its design derived from French châteaux and Flemish guild halls, was opened in 1868 for the 'sons of tradesmen and persons of the working class generally whose parents stand in the need of assistance.' The School Board purchased the Hospital buildings and opened them as a day school in 1889, with 650 pupils and fifteen teachers. However, the decision was made to build a new school and the current Harris Academy was erected on the Perth Road in 1931.

The independent High School of Dundee, local authority-run Morgan Academy and Harris Academy endure, preserving high educational standards. At the same time there are other secondary, primary and nursery schools in the city staffed by dedicated teachers, employing innovative techniques in an age in which academic qualifications are becoming more and more important. Latin may have lost its status in the curriculum, but other languages and the sciences give Dundee's adolescents an international perspective.

The pupils of Ancrum Road Primary School recreate a Victorian classroom in Dundee. There are inkwells in the desks, old money on the blackboard, and the teacher with pointer (for rapping on bonneted heads giving the wrong answer: not allowed nowadays!) is actually one of the pupils. Other schools visit for a lesson in living history.

They look very mature for primary pupils as they converse on the splendid staircase of the High School of Dundee.

Rapt concentration and exuberance from part of the brass section of the Harris Academy wind band during a rehearsal in the school hall for a concert.

Who would believe, looking at the splendid edifice of Morgan Academy, that it suffered a catastrophic fire in March 2001? Only the external façade was left standing after the blaze, which took fire fighters 17 hours to put out. But with assistance from Historic Scotland, Dundee City Council, and the restoration skills of Mansell Construction Company, £17 million was spent returning the school to its former elegance.

Against a pleasing integration of the original building and a light and airy modern extension, Stephen Shaw, Rector of Morgan Academy, chats to pupils.

'They shall not grow old': Armistice Parade,
High School of Dundee.

University of Dundee

It was a momentous day for Dundee when Mary Ann Baxter of Balgavies put on her bonnet and instructed her coachman to take her to the office of her lawyer John Boyd Baxter. This was going to be an extraordinary gesture of philanthropy by a member of the Baxter mill dynasty. Both Miss Baxter and John Boyd Baxter wanted to found a college of higher learning, and she was prepared to back their dream with a draft for £120,000 – a sum equivalent to several millions in today's money. John Boyd Baxter gave £5,000. She later gave an extra £10,000 and he pledged a further £5,000.

The deed establishing the College stated that it would provide teaching in science, literature and the arts to persons of both sexes and that no one was to be required to reveal his or her religious belief or that any religious teaching was to be introduced.

University College opened in October 1883, having acquired four detached town houses on the Nethergate. Various purchases of land and existing property as well as new building projects expanded the College north from the Nethergate and west.

Two of the most famous professors attracted to Dundee were D'Arcy Wentworth Thompson and Patrick Geddes. A statistician, biologist, mathematician and ecologist, D'Arcy Wentworth Thompson's worldwide travels allowed him to amass one of the finest zoological collections of its day. The botanist Patrick Geddes developed his interests in sociology and town planning when he was appointed to Dundee.

A Faculty of Medicine was established in 1897 and a Dental Hospital founded in 1914. In 1890 University College Dundee was affiliated to the University of St Andrews, and in 1897, officially incorporated as a college of the University of St Andrews.

In 1954 University College Dundee changed its constitution and its name to Queen's College, which in 1967, by Royal Charter, became the University of Dundee and an independent university after a 70 year relationship (sometimes stormy) with the University of St Andrews.

In 1996 the University of Dundee absorbed the two local nursing colleges to create a single School of Nursing and Midwifery within the Faculty of Medicine and Dentistry, and in 1994 it merged with its next door neighbour Duncan of Jordanstone College of Art. The University's most recent merger was with the Dundee campus of Northern College in late 2001, to create a seventh faculty, that of a Faculty of Education and Social Work.

The University of Dundee has nearly 15,000 students (including 9,500 full-time undergraduates) across seven faculties and an international reputation in many areas of excellence. It attracts students from all over the world, which would have delighted that intrepid traveller Professor D'Arcy Wentworth Thompson.

Sir Alan Langlands, FRSE, Principal and Vice-Chancellor, in the procession of a medical graduation ceremony at the University of Dundee. Sir Alan was the Chief Executive of the National Health Service in England from 1994-2000 where, as the Secretary of State's principal policy adviser for the NHS, he was accountable to Parliament for the effective stewardship of a £42billion revenue budget. He has an international reputation in the development of healthcare policy and as a strategic manager of health services. He has advised in many countries, including Russia, the USA, Canada and China.

The exquisite mace of the University of Dundee was given to University College Dundee by the President of the Dundee Chamber of Commerce, to commemorate the 500th anniversary of the University of St Andrews (of which UCD was then a College) in 1911. The mace was designed by Thomas Delgaty Dunn, the first full-time teacher of art at the Dundee Technical Institute, then head of the Art School when that expanded to become Dundee Technical College and School of Art. The mace was made by William B. Smith of Glasgow, with the figures of Law, St Mary and Medicine modelled by William Vickers.

Fraser Millar, President of the University of Dundee Students' Association, Vice-President Lianne Bibby, and, in the middle, the Rector, the broadcasting personality Lorraine Kelly, relax in the elegant setting of the Geddes Quadrangle.

Getting down to study in the library of the University of Dundee.

Caroline Brown, Deputy Archivist, University of Dundee Archive Services, examines a unique volume, 'Illustrations of Scottish Flora, chiefly of Forfarshire and Fifeshire,' written, compiled and illustrated by David Robert Robertson between 1912 and 1914. The volume is one of the many treasures in the University's archives.

The Geddes Quadrangle, named after University College's Professor Patrick Geddes.

The late Queen Elizabeth became Chancellor of the University of Dundee when it gained independent status in 1967, so it is appropriate that the Queen Mother Research Centre should be concerned with the use of computer technology for older people.

Reflecting the past at the University of Dundee: the Harris Building, part of the Geddes Quadrangle, was built in 1909 for Engineering, and later taken over for Physics.

The Students' Union of the University of Dundee offers many activities, from e-mailing friends to karaoke.

Treasures from the University of Dundee's Zoology Museum in the elegant form of Huia birds. Now extinct, it was a type of wattle bird, found only in New Zealand's North Island. The male and female birds were unique in having different bill shapes. Biologists surmise that they may have worked together as a pair, the male pulling apart bark or wood while the female used her long curved bill to extract grubs, a rare example of the equal division of labour between the sexes.

This King Penguin surveying the shore at Broughty Ferry was presented to D'Arcy Thompson by Sir Ernest Shackleton who brought it back from his 1907-09 expedition to the South Pole, during which he reached within 97 miles of the Pole.

University of Dundee graduates have a lot to smile about.

Professor Sir James Black, CH, Nobel Laureate, Chancellor of the University of Dundee from 1992 to 2006 and one of the world's greatest scientists, confers a degree in dentistry on Muna Al-Balushi.

University of Dundee students ride high at their graduation ball.

Medicine in Dundee

You are a Dundonian in need of medical attention in the sixteenth century, and are directed down a wynd to a barber's shop. Surely there is some mistake. But the barber also practises as a surgeon, and as he picks up the rusty open razor you feel faint.

You need some Latin to read about Dr David Kinloch, one of Dundee's greatest medical sons, whose monument in the Howff has a Latin panegyric to 'a most skilful physician to the Kings of Great Britain and France.' In Madrid, while trying to secure the betrothal of the Infanta for the future Charles 1, on the instructions of King James V1, whose 'Medicinar' he was, Dr Kinloch was thrown into prison as a heretic, where he apparently sent through the bars of his cell a black cat with a message tied to its tail to cure the Grand Inquisitor of a strange illness. Kinloch's life was spared, and he returned to Dundee, to write poems in Latin on medical themes.

When a travelling elephant collapsed and expired on the Ferry Road in 1706, Dr Patrick Blair, another noted Dundee physician, carried out a dissection in front of a large crowd under a fierce sun. Elephants were probably better treated than humans in an era without a state medical service, when life and death depended on the number of pennies in one's purse.

The first patients were admitted to the King Street Infirmary in 1798, but within decades it proved to be inadequate. In 1855 the new Infirmary (the Royal) to the east of Dudhope Castle opened, then King's Cross Hospital in 1889.

At the end of the nineteenth century, with the establishment at St Andrews University of a medical school, Dundee Royal Infirmary became a teaching hospital, with women holding medical chairs. In 1898 a Conjoint Medical School was established at Dundee.

Ninewells Hospital and Medical School was completed in 1974, and is a town by itself in a pleasant location on the outskirts of the city. Over the past thirty years it has developed an envied reputation in many branches of medicine, and is noted for its research as well as its sympathetic patient care.

It is a tribute to the excellence of medical research in Dundee that the Wellcome Trust established its Biocentre in the city in 1997. It was built and equipped with donations totalling over £13 million, including £10 million from The Wellcome Trust, thought to be the largest single charitable donation ever given to a Scottish institution. This international centre of medical excellence houses over 200 scientists and support staff, and attracts massive research funds.

Large medicine chests were awkward to convey in a horse-drawn coach or trap, so nineteenth century physicians often carried pocket-sized versions for use in emergencies. The owner of this compact set was Sir James Young Simpson, the celebrated Edinburgh obstetrician who introduced chloroform as an anaesthetic in 1847. Sir James gave this medicine box to his friend Dr James Ross of Inverness, and in 1884 Dr Ross's widow gave the box to the father of Major General Douglas Wimberley, Principal of University College Dundee from 1946-54. It is now in the Tayside Medical History Museum.

When the owner of this microscope, which is now in the Tayside Medical History Museum, died in 1903, it was said that he 'deserves a niche in the Temple of Fame as one of the great benefactors of the human race.' Dr Thomas Maclagan was medical superintendent at Dundee Royal Infirmary from 1864-66. A major fever epidemic led this brilliant physician to pioneer the clinical use of thermometers. His most enduring legacy was his research into the anti-rheumatic effects of salicin, a chemical extracted from willow bark. Maclagan's work was advanced by German researchers who used salicin to develop acetyl-salicylic acid – better known today as aspirin.

Sir Philip Cohen, FRS, Royal Society Research Professor, and Director, MRC Protein Phosphorylation Unit & Wellcome Trust Biocentre at the University of Dundee, checks data with doctoral student Sarah Conner. His research into the role of protein phosphorylation in human health and disease is world famous and of profound significance.

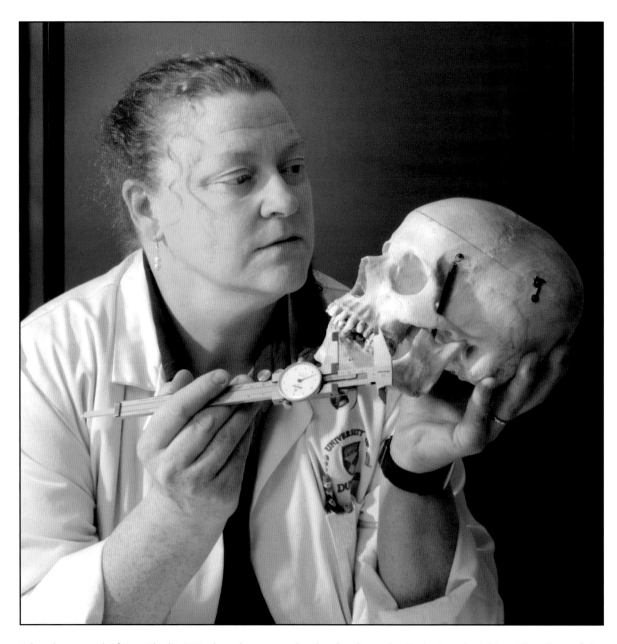

It has been said of Sue Black, OBE, that she can make the dead speak, disclosing their identities. One of the foremost forensic anthropologists in the world, this self-effacing University of Dundee professor has worked on cases as diverse as trying to match human remains to Lord Lucan, to painstaking and sensitive research for the International War Crimes Tribunal on bodies found in mass graves in Kosovo, so that families may know the fate of their loved ones.

Completed in 1974, Ninewells Hospital has been described as a 'medical New Town.' A teaching hospital for the University of Dundee, it offers superb standards of service.

Ninewells Hospital, centre for care and research.

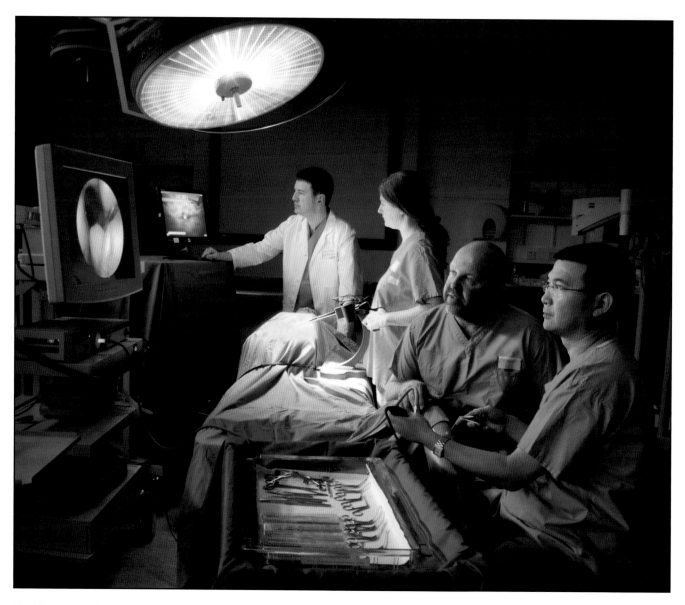

Healthcare workers training in the Cuschieri Skills Centre, located at Ninewells Hospital, named after Sir Alfred Cuschieri, FRSE, Professor of Surgery, Ninewells Hospital and Medical School. Sir Alfred is an international pioneer and a major exponent of minimal invasive surgery ('keyhole surgery'). The centre was opened in 1992 and set up to provide specialized training for medical staff and other healthcare professionals. New developments in techniques and equipment require skills to be updated continually to ensure the best outcome for the patient. Using state-of-the-art facilities, the staff of the Cuschieri Skills Centre design training packages to meet these changing requirements. The combination of virtual reality, interventional human anatomy, custom-built skills laboratories and a simulated operating theatre means that this centre is one of the most innovative training facilities in Europe.

A quiet conversation in 'a friendly little clubhouse,' as the world renowned architect Frank Gehry described his first building in the United Kingdom, erected in Dundee. Inspirational in every way, Maggie's Centre, which was opened in 2003, is a tribute to the courage and compassion of the architect's close friend the late Maggie Keswick Jencks, a cancer sufferer who founded a patient-support programme, with its first centre in Edinburgh.

Dundee's Maggie's Centre, in the grounds of Ninewells Hospital, is a haven where cancer patients from the nearby hospital, as well as their friends and families, can meet to share experiences and to obtain information for services that complement medical treatment. The small tower that dominates the project was inspired by lighthouses – the beacon of hope.

Duncan of Jordanstone College of Art and Design

Towards the end of the nineteenth century students carrying boxes of paints and freshly laundered smocks could be seen making their way to Small's Wynd, where the Technical Institute, opened in 1888, incorporated an art school, with Thomas Delgaty Dunn appointed the first full-time art master in 1892.

By 1905 the building was becoming seriously overcrowded with lathes and easels, so funds were raised to move to new premises on Bell Street. The building was completed in 1911, and was renamed the Dundee Technical College & School of Art.

In 1909 James Duncan of Jordanstone bequeathed £60,000 towards founding an independent art school in Dundee, but it took until the 1930s to finalize plans for a new College on Perth Road. War delayed the construction, and when built in 1953-64 the original design – the result of a competition – had been altered. The adjacent Matthew Building for the College was designed in 1974 and has been praised as having 'an interior quality…as high as can be found anywhere else in Scotland.'

A Committee of Enquiry debated if the existing structure of the Dundee Institute of Art and Technology should be maintained, or if the two disciplines would be better served through the establishment of two independent colleges. The Dundee Institute of Art and Technology was dissolved in 1975 to create Dundee College of Technology and Duncan of Jordanstone College of Art. The Art College remained independent under its own Board of Governors until 1994, when it became a full faculty of the University of Dundee.

The University of Dundee and the College worked together, with the result that by 1988 all degree courses at Duncan of Jordanstone College of Art were validated by the University of Dundee. The College has expanded to become the largest college of art and design in Scotland, offering a huge range of courses, including architecture, regional planning, environmental management, painting, sculpture, printmaking, printed textiles, graphic design, ceramics, jewellery, metalwork, food and welfare studies, hotel and catering management and hospitality.

Additional postgraduate areas of study available within the College are computer-aided architectural design, electronic imaging, film and television production and European urban conservation.

Duncan of Jordanstone has distinguished graduates and teachers. The sculptor David Mach, who uses mass-produced objects, most notably magazines, newspapers and car tyres, has had exhibitions all over the world and, is, appropriately, Professor of Inspiration and Discovery at the College. Award-winning artist Calum Colvin completed a diploma in Sculpture at the College in 1983 and is a part-time lecturer there. For his work, which often combines photography, sculpture and painting to striking effect, he has received the OBE. In the younger generation the work of Yong Hoon Choi from South Korea investigates shadows, light and the human body translated into startling sculptures.

Graham Little, one of Britain's most successful artists who has Broughty Ferry connections, also studied at Duncan of Jordanstone. He has said: 'I'm trying to make something that holds people's attention for as long as possible. I don't know why you'd want that, but it's definitely always been a desire for me. You can't see my sculptures all at once, so you've got to use your memory a bit.'

Rose Borthwick must love birds. Eighty one of them adorn her work, which, she insists, 'is not painting. The background colour is paint, but the birds themselves are black matt vinyl stickers. I drew all the birds and then scanned them and tried to add the right scale of the birds and took the files to a sign maker in Dundee and they cut them into vinyl.' Rose's avian work featured in her final degree display at Duncan of Jordanstone College of Art and Design. Destined to be a high flier, she won a Scottish Royal Academy scholarship which took her to Florence.

Richard Foley working on a print by Harry Gillan at Duncan of Jordanstone College of Art and Design.

A study in concentration as Jiang Luyi prepares for her final presentation at Duncan of Jordanstone College of Art and Design.

University of Abertay Dundee

'Through the foundation of this Institute…the ladder of learning has been raised aloft in Dundee,' a speaker said proudly at the opening of the Dundee Technical Institute on 15 October 1888. Over two hundred eager students had carried their books down Small's Wynd into the specially designed building on 6 September of that year.

The Institute was given the responsibility of organising evening classes in Dundee, and had to move to new premises on Bell Street which were to become the Dundee Technical College & School of Art in 1911. By 1946 the Institute was recognized by the University of London and in 1951 it awarded its external degrees to the Institute's graduates in pharmacy, mechanical engineering, civil engineering and electrical engineering. In 1955 a new department of management and higher commercial studies was added to the Institute's provision, offering courses approved by the British Institute of Management.

By 1975 the Institute had become one of the major non-university institutions of higher education in Scotland. The School of Art had moved into new premises on Perth Road, leading to the creation of two separate institutions: the Duncan of Jordanstone College of Art, and the Dundee College of Technology with its Bell Street site significantly expanded.

The Institute became the first in Scotland to offer a science-based degree course in nursing, and was ahead of the times in offering a Higher Diploma in Computing in 1980. In April 1994 the Institute became the University of Abertay Dundee. Its Specialist Centres include: Pain Management Research Centre; and Abertay Centre for the Environment. Other centres include the SIMBIOS bioinformatics research centre and IC CAVE, an international computer games research centre.

Abertay is best known for its digital media, creative industries and environmental science teaching and research. It was the first university in the world to offer computer games technology degrees (now copied by more than 60 other UK universities). The University is a leader in distance learning, with around 650 off-campus students located elsewhere in Scotland, and also in Europe and in Asia.

The University now embraces four academic Schools: Computing & Creative Technologies, Contemporary Sciences, Social & Health Sciences, and the Dundee Business School.

The University is conveniently located on a city centre campus, with all of its buildings within a quarter of a mile of each other. Shops, recreational facilities and the main bus and train stations are a short walk away. The main buildings, Old College, Kydd Building and others, are in the Bell Street complex grouped around the University's outstanding award-winning Library. These buildings house the majority of teaching departments, the University's administrative offices, student refectory, research centres, and library.

No one wants to leave the new Student Centre at the University of Abertay Dundee, because it has everything: an exhibition gallery and theatre/cinema, a bar/bistro, another bar, a nightclub, a snack-bar and a shop as well as social space and events space.

This is a serious academic exercise, not a student taking a break. University of Abertay Dundee researcher Prasada Kuna studies the screen in IC CAVE's computer games usability laboratory.

The University of Abertay Dundee's stylish library.

The reflective peace of the University of Abertay Dundee's library.

Abertay tree in jar: researcher Angie McHugh, from the University's Plant Biotechnology Research Group, pictured tending cloned elm trees as part of a project to devise a green solution to Dutch Elm Disease.

Dundee's kilted Lord Provost John Letford follows the mace of the University of Abertay Dundee during a graduation ceremony.

A proud male doctoral graduate of the University of Abertay Dundee chats to two members of staff.

University of Abertay Dundee graduates mingle with proud parents and families.

Happy Bachelor of Science graduates from the University of Abertay Dundee's School of Social & Health Sciences, with a party going on in the background, it seems.

Dundee College

Youngsters with gifted feet are heading for the Scottish School of Contemporary Dance at Dundee College to train in The Space, a £5 million dance, theatre and conference centre, part funded by the Scottish Arts Council's National Lottery Fund and located on the College's Kingsway Campus.

The custom-built facility for the Scottish School of Contemporary Dance at the Kingsway Campus was officially opened by Her Majesty the Queen in 2002. Not only does this facility offer a superb environment for students of both contemporary dance and theatre arts: it has become an established venue for top-flight dance companies on tour. In the past few years Scottish Ballet, the X factor Dance Company, Scottish Dance Theatre, the David Hughes Dance Company, and the Stephen Petronio Company of New York, have all performed at The Space. But as well as performing, all of these companies have conducted workshops and masterclasses with students, offering them a unique opportunity to work with established professional dancers.

Dundee College was created in 1986 from a merger of the former Dundee College of Commerce, sited on Constitution Road, and Kingsway Technical College at the junction of Kingsway and Old Glamis Road. Dundee College came outwith local authority control through incorporation in 1993, which resulted in 43 further education colleges in Scotland leaving the administration of the local authority (at that time Regional Councils) and reporting directly to the Scottish Office. College Principals, instead of reporting to the Director of Education, became responsible to a special board of management unique to their own college.

During the following decade Dundee College successfully embarked on a programme of expansion both in numbers of students and the variety of courses on offer. Operating out of four sites across the city – Constitution Campus, Kingsway Campus, Graham Street Campus and Melrose Campus – the College has grown in scale and reputation, particularly in the cultural and creative areas.

The College has Centres of Excellence in Automotive Technology and in Plumbing and Gas Central Heating. Construction trades are a priority at the College which launched a ground-breaking initiative in 2002, enabling S3 pupils to come into College to gain experience in a number of trades. Working closely with local businesses the Construction Apprentice Training Initiative guarantees apprenticeships for those pupils who successfully complete this two-year programme.

Hospitality and catering students now work in a totally refurbished environment at the Kingsway Campus, including a state-of-the-art training restaurant. As part of the drive to encourage training in tourism students are offered paid work placements with employers in this growing industry.

Science, particularly bioscience, has also become a growth area at Dundee College. In 2003 a brand-new bioscience laboratory was opened at the Kingsway Campus. A second lab was brought on-line in 2005.

Dundee College's Constitution campus situated on Constitution Road.

The elegant exterior of The Space Dance and Theatre facility at Dundee College, Kingsway Campus.

Greer Campbell and Kim Brymer performing in work choreographed by Sindy Monson in The Space Dance facility at Dundee College.

Elizabeth Rawes performing in work
choreographed by Karen Thompson
in The Space Dance facility.

Is the bride about to commit murder? Ruth Darbyshire and Iain Leslie in a production as part of the HNC Acting & Performance Course at Dundee College.

Professor Abd al-Fattah El-Awaisi, Principal and Vice-Chancellor of Dundee's Al-Maktoum Institute, one of the country's leading academics in the history of Islams and Muslims, is the author of an important monograph offering a model for peaceful co-existence and mutual respect in Islamicjerusalem. Professor El-Awaisi has also done much to promote multiculturalism in Scotland in general and Dundee in particular.

This evocative painting by Eddie Lange shows Dundee's *Discovery* ship and Dubai's *Arab Dhow* moving towards each other. The painting symbolizes the twinning of the two cities, and the effort by the Al-Maktoum Institute in building bridges between communities and people. The logo of the Institute, which both cities share, is in the water and on the sides of the ships.

Postgraduate students studying at the Al-Maktoum Institute. The one at the front is Rana Al-Soufi, who is doing a Master of Literature degree in Islamicjerusalem Studies. The student at the back is Mandy McKeral, who is preparing a PhD in the Study of Islam and Muslims.

A Dandy Firm

Magic didn't start with Harry Potter. Long before the boy wizard, the antics of certain characters in the comics of D.C. Thomson & Co. Ltd were keeping children enthralled, and a week without a comic was a week of misery for parents and offspring alike.

It was a fortunate day in the 1870s when William Thomson, a Dundee ship-owner, launched himself into publishing by taking shares in a local firm which published the *Dundee Courier and Argus* (founded 1816) and the *Weekly News* (1855). When William gained full control of the firm in 1886, his son D. C. Thomson became his partner, and over the years nephews were taken on as fully committed partners. There was something of a newspaper war in Dundee between W. and D. C. Thomson and the bigger firm of John Leng & Co. Ltd, publishers of the *Dundee Advertiser* (1801), the *Dundee Evening Telegraph* (1877), the *People's Journal* (1858) and the *People's Friend* (1869).

In 1906 the two businesses came together, with Thomson's as the majority partner, and, inevitably, as owners. In 1926 after the General Strike the *Dundee Advertiser* merged with the *Courier*, which today has the biggest sale of any provincial newspaper in the UK.

Have you ever come across an old paper, the *Post Sunday Special*, in the attic, or under old linoleum? You should have kept this collector's item, because it was launched in Glasgow in 1914 and became the *Sunday Post*, which has been in the *Guinness Book of Records* as the 'most read newspaper'.

D.C. Thomson created great comics. It all began in 1921 with the *Adventure, a* story paper in text form for boys. 1937 is a date so many children should be grateful for. That was the year when the *Dandy* first appeared, and the following year, the *Beano*. Thomson knew what their readers wanted, which is why the *Weekly News* sold over a million copies each week. There are *Friendship Books* on shelves throughout the land, and adults still add to the comic annuals they started collecting as children. In fact, early comics in good condition (rare, because you wanted to go back to them again and again while eating a jeelie piece) fetch big prices.

Some newspaper owners are acquisitive, but D. C. Thomson have never coveted other people's papers. Their only acquisition was the *Scots Magazine,* which they purchased in 1927 (believe it or not, it was first published in 1739).

Publishers of fifteen titles encompassing newspapers, magazines and comics – 200 million copies in total each year to instruct and delight all ages – D.C. Thomson & Co. Ltd are a Dundee phenomenon.

The *Evening Telegraph* rolls off the press at D.C. Thomson's Kingsway printing works. The paper has been bringing news to the citizens of Dundee since 1877.

Studio artist Jimmy Glen works on Dennis the Menace and Gnasher, two of the best loved characters from D.C. Thomson's school of fun.

Jimmy Dewar prepares a caricature using a scanned computer image at D.C. Thomson's, renowned for their investment in the most up-to-date equipment and talent to bring us laughs and drama galore.

The National Cash Register Company came to Dundee after the war, and by 1969 was handing out 6,000 pay packets in seven factories round the city. Following decimalization the workforce was reduced drastically. But NCR has endured in Dundee. NCR Corporation is a $6 billion global market leader active in over 100 countries and territories, and its Kingsway West site in Dundee is the Corporation's main Scottish facility, where NCR designs, develops, manufactures and markets state-of-the-art self-service solutions. NCR's leading-edge technology extends beyond hole-in-the-wall cash dispensers to machines which can recognize customers from the unique pattern of the iris and respond to transaction requests by speech recognition and synthesis.

Sean Devlin checks a product at the Michelin Tyre plc factory at Baldovie Road, Dundee.

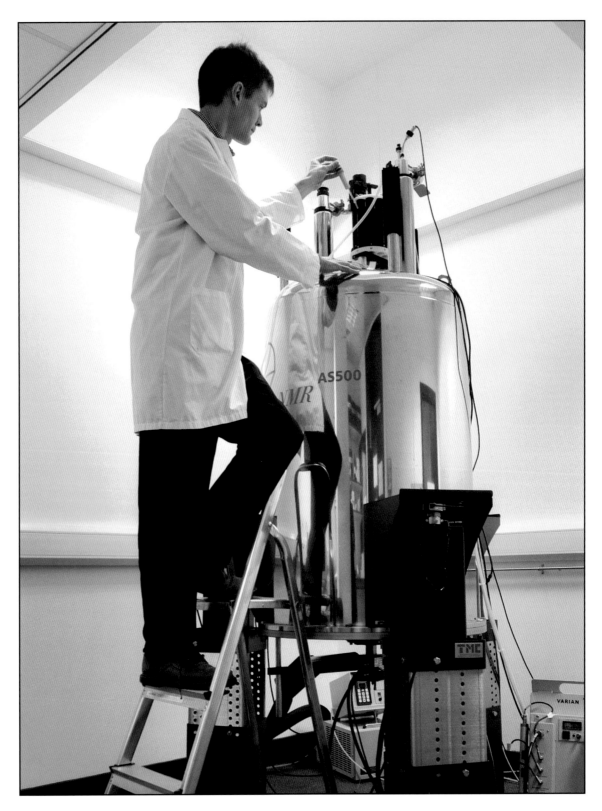

Dr Campbell McInnes inspects a process at the plant of Cyclacel Ltd., James Lindsay Place, Dundee. Co-founded by Professor Sir David Lane, whose team from the University of Dundee discovered the P53 gene (the so-called tumour suppressor gene), Cyclacel's international team is involved in research and development at its custom-built premises.

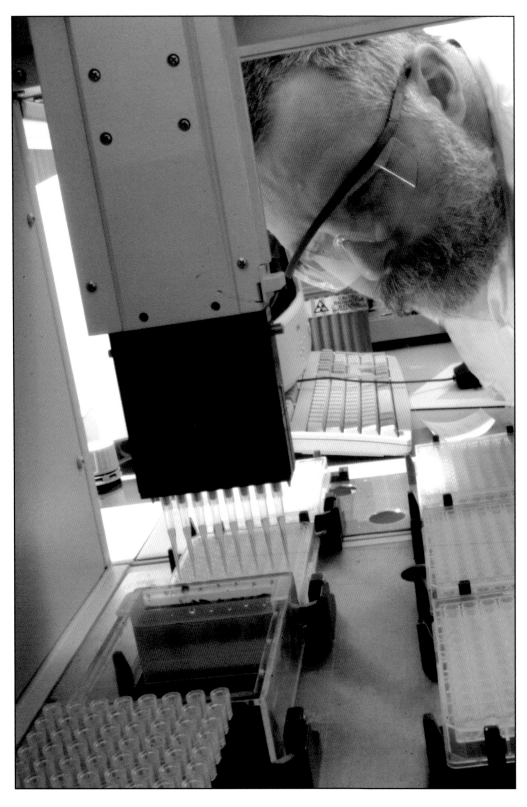

Dr Andrew Johnston of Upstate Ltd., founded in Dundee in 1999, part of Upstate Incorporated in Charlottesville, Virginia. The company is growing rapidly and already employs nearly 40 people. The sales of University of Dundee products by Upstate run into millions of pounds.

As its name implies, the Phoenix at 103 Nethergate has had several reincarnations. Dating from at least the nineteenth century, and probably earlier, around the period preceding the First World War it was known as Fenwick's Bar, after Peter Fenwick the proprietor.

Following his death in 1952 it became The Town and Gown. The present genial host, Alan Bannerman, has owned the Phoenix since 1986, and won awards for its selection of real ales.

Named after the old townhouse which was demolished in 1932, the Pillars, a Scottish & Newcastle plc tenanted bar at 9 Crichton Street, has a model of the townhouse above its door, and inside, a warm welcome, when a dram aids the circulation – and conversation – on chilly days by the Tay.

Dundee goes continental: the market in Reform Street with its plants to brighten city homes is held several times a year.

Covered arcades are part of Dundee's history, but surely the Overgate Centre is an exceptional experience. Set against a spectacular curved glass wall, the only single-sided mall in Europe houses some of the most famous fashion brands in the world. As you sip your cappuccino in one of the Overgate's stylish cafés, reflect that it was called Argylisgait, and was the main western route out of ancient Dundee, and (with your credit card balance in mind), the traditional site of a Royal Mint.

The illuminated office of the Bank of Scotland in the Nethergate.

Star-struck in the Wellgate Shopping Centre, built on the site of an old shopping street named Wellgate which linked the residential Hilltown to the north and the prime traditional shopping street in Dundee named Murraygate to the south. The name Wellgate derives from the old Scots 'wellgait,' which means the walk to the well; in this case the walk from Dundee city centre to collect water from Our Lady's Well which was situated to the north of the Wellgate.

The enchantment of the Wellgate: on the hour the doors open on the ornamental clock, and some children will swear that the unicorn moves.

A gilded elephant crosses the floor in the Forum, one of Yvonne Brown's Keiller's china shops in Dundee, where today's gifts are tomorrow's antiques.

Ally Bally (Arthur Ballingall), managing director of Radio Tay, has been broadcasting to Tayside, Angus and North East Fife for years, and now has his daughter Karen with him in the studio to keep the listeners entertained and informed.

Tayside Police

You wouldn't have wanted to be in Dundee in the closing days of March 1831, during the illumination in honour of the success of the Reform Bill, when, the *Scotsman* reported with relish, 'a scene of violence, tumult, and outrage' took place. 'The Constables and the Police were assailed with showers of stones, and driven down the lane which leads to the Police Office. In the course of the skirmishes, forty of the crowd were seized, and put into the Cells.'

The violence continued, and on the following day… 'a boat with a barrel of tar in it, was drawn up the Murraygate, and kindled below the Piazzas of the Gaol, whereby the Justices and others in the Council-Room, ran some risk of being suffocated by the smoke. The Police Office was then assailed; the door was burst open by means of a beam of wood, used as a battering-ram; the Superintendent of Police, and others who were in the Office at the time, made their escape by a back way; the prisoners were released; the Police Office was sacked; the Superintendent's books, the greater part of the furniture, the benches of the Courtroom, the watchmen's great coats, rattles, &c were thrown out into the lane, and burned in a heap before the door. The town was completely in the hands of the mob…'

Today, helpful police officers of both sexes watch for signs of trouble through closed circuit television cameras, and patrol the streets – a far cry from the turbulent times of the Reform Bill riots, when a party of the 78th Highlanders had to be dispatched from Perth to help to restore order.

Tayside Fire Service

You can hear the clatter of the hooves hauling the appliance through the streets, smoke making the horses snort, the din of bells deafening them. 'Dreadful Conflagration in Dundee' was the headline in the *Scotsman* for Wednesday 6 January 1841. 'On Sunday morning last, about five o' clock, a fire was discovered in a portion of the venerable pile of buildings which has for many centuries been the pride and ornament of the town. The alarm was instantly given to the police by the person whose duty it is to light the stoves for heating the churches. Shortly afterwards the fire brigade, with the engines, and the military from the Barracks, hurried to the spot, and the alarm-bells pealed forth to rouse the inhabitants, hundreds of whom hastened from all parts of the town in the direction of the flames. About half-past six the conflagration was at its height – the three churches, from their base to the highest pinnacle, being one mass of fire...the ancient Tower, which rises to the height of 156 feet, attached to the Steeple Church, the only one not in flames, rose Phoenix like above the contention, the peal of bells in its interior imparting a mournful grandeur to the spectacle.'

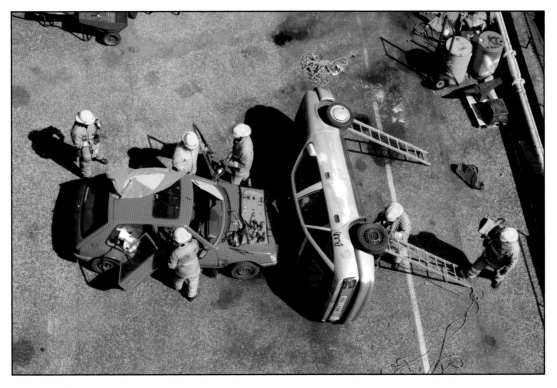

Tayside Fire Service continues to serve the city of Dundee. Computers and the most modern appliances, as well as constant training exercises, ensure that the helmeted heroes reach the site of fires and accidents within minutes despite the complicated road and street lay-out.

Dundee Treasures on display

Dr Patrick Blair founded the city's first museum, the Hall of Rarities and Physik Garden, at the beginning of the eighteenth century. Then in 1824 the Watt Institution was established, named after the famous steam engineer. Working men were educated in the building in Constitution Road which also mounted exhibitions. But the foundation of the Albert Institute was the real beginning of a museum service fit for Dundee.

The original purpose of the building, which would become known as the McManus Galleries, was as a monument to Queen Victoria's beloved consort Prince Albert, who died in 1861. Once again the philanthropists of the city reached for their cheque books, with Sir David 'Jute' Baxter donating £10,000 to the project. Prince Albert was to be commemorated by establishing an institute dedicated to science, literature, and the arts and crafts.

Sir George Gilbert Scott was chosen to design the building, and by 1867 it had been completed and named the Albert Institute. The building contained a new public library and a banqueting hall which later became the reference library.

In 1873 a local architect, David MacKenzie, completed an extension to provide space for a museum, permanent art gallery, and temporary exhibitions.

In celebration of Queen Victoria's Golden Jubilee in 1887 the art lobby in the city raised funds for a further extension to the Museum and Art Galleries. James Guthrie Orchar, the prime mover, designed the barrel-vaulted art galleries with their unique curved walls. The City Architect William Alexander oversaw the Victoria Galleries, which were completed in 1889. This extension was the last major external alteration to the building.

The Public Museum, Library and Art Gallery continued to expand during the twentieth century. Some internal adjustments were made occasionally, but it was not until 1978 that the Albert Institute entered a new phase. The Public Library moved to new premises in the Wellgate Centre, and the Albert Institute / Victoria Galleries was taken over completely by the Art Gallery and Museum. There were further occasional internal alternations during the 1980s and 1990s.

In May 1984 the Albert Institute was renamed the McManus Galleries in honour of former Lord Provost Dr. Maurice McManus who had died in 1982 at the age of 75 after a long and distinguished career in local politics.

Closed for refurbishment for two years at time of writing, the McManus Galleries and Museum will give Dundee a space fit for the twenty first century to display artistic treasures, as well as more prosaic items associated with the history of the city.

Sir George Gilbert Scott's Albert Institute of 1865-67, built in Dundee in memory of Queen Victoria's beloved consort. The architect wrote of his design for Glasgow University: 'I adopted a style which I may call my own invention having already initiated it at the Albert Institute in Dundee. It is simply a thirteenth- or fourteenth-century secular style, with the addition of certain Scottish features peculiar in that country in the sixteenth century...' The Albert Institute houses the McManus Galleries and Museum.

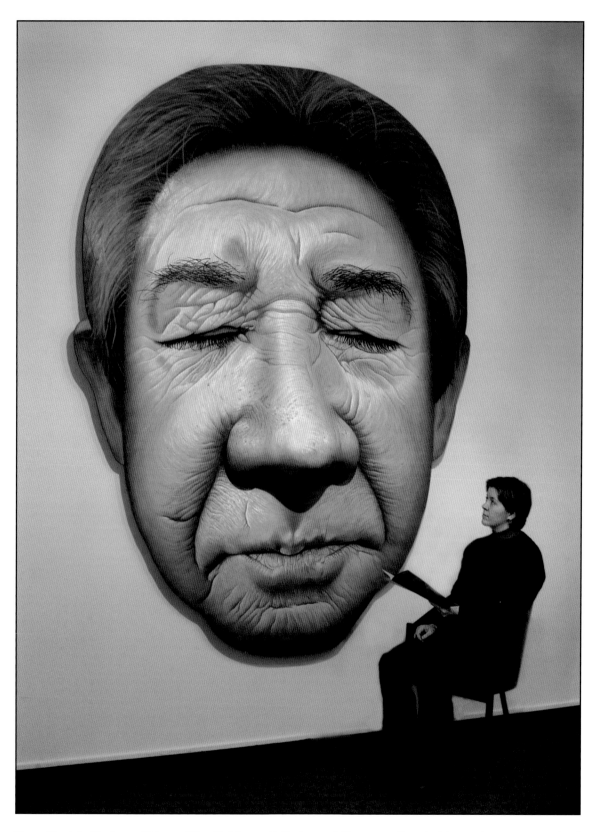

Fiona Sinclair, Heritage Officer of the McManus Galleries and Museum, sits admiring a close-up portrait of his father by the artist Simon Reekie (born 1974). The Museum acquired the picture in 2004.

An evocative study of Highland cattle in the mist by the artist Peter Graham (1836-1921), immensely popular in his day. Evidently he had to have cattle brought to him so that he could paint them in comparative comfort.

The astrolabe in the McManus collection dates from 1555. Unlike other navigational tools it takes its point from above.

The stained glass window of Mary Slessor in the Museum was designed by William Aikman of London and paid for by the Dundee community, in memory of the Dundee mill worker whose selfless labours in Nigeria as a missionary and teacher earned her the name 'Mother of All the Peoples.' She died, exhausted of fever in 1915, and the window was erected in the Museum in 1923 to a woman with saintly qualities.

The Beautiful Game in Dundee

Children must have dribbled balls down the wynds of Dundee for generations, but the game of football began in earnest in the city in 1893, when Dundee Football Club was formed by an amalgamation of two city teams, Our Boys and East End. Who possesses a souvenir programme of the Club's first Scottish League game on Saturday, 12 August 1893, which resulted in a 3-3 draw against Glasgow Rangers at West Craigie Park, home of Our Boys? That same season saw the Club transfer to more modern facilities at Carolina Port but, in December 1898, a financial crisis almost closed down the Club. However, local business supporters and the ordinary people of Dundee gave financial and vocal support, and in August 1899, the Club's new ground at Dens Park was officially opened.

The boardroom at Dens Park displays the honours of over a century of top class football: the Scottish Cup in 1910; the League Cup in 1951, 1952 and 1973; and under the guidance of the legendary Bob Shankly, the First Division Championship in 1962. Mention Alan Gilzean, and Dundee F.C. supporters will recall the balls he put away to help the Club to reach the semi final of the European Cup.

Dundee businessmen Peter and James Marr took control of the Club in 1997, and with the appointment of Jocky Scott as Manager, and the signing of several key players the Club was promoted to the newly formed Scottish Premier League. New stands and new players at Dens Park have brought Dundee F.C. with confidence into the new millennium.

Dundee's other great team came into being in 1909, when the Irish community banded together to form a football club following the demise of Dundee Harp three years earlier. They initially called themselves Dundee Hibernian and took over Clepington Park, the home of Dundee Wanderers, thus displacing the previous occupants. Clepington Park was renamed Tannadice Park, a venue that would rank with Ibrox and Parkhead.

In February 1913 Dundee Hibs kicked off a long association with the Scottish Cup, losing 4-2 to Queen's Park at Hampden. In 1923, in a bid for wider appeal, the club decided to drop the reference to Hibernian from their title. Dundee City was their favoured choice but this led to a protest by city rivals Dundee. Ultimately the name of Dundee United was adopted.

Dundee United has had great managers. Jerry Kerr's appointment in 1959 brought the club back into the First Division. He was succeeded by Jim McLean in 1971, opening the most successful era in the club's history. The zenith of their achievements in Europe came in 1986-87 when United became the first Scottish club to reach the final of the UEFA Cup. Dundee United continues to be a formidable opponent at home and abroad.

Eddie Thompson, popular Chairman of Dundee United, autographs programmes for two mascots at Tannadice Park.

Barry Smith, Captain, Dundee F.C., displays his skills.

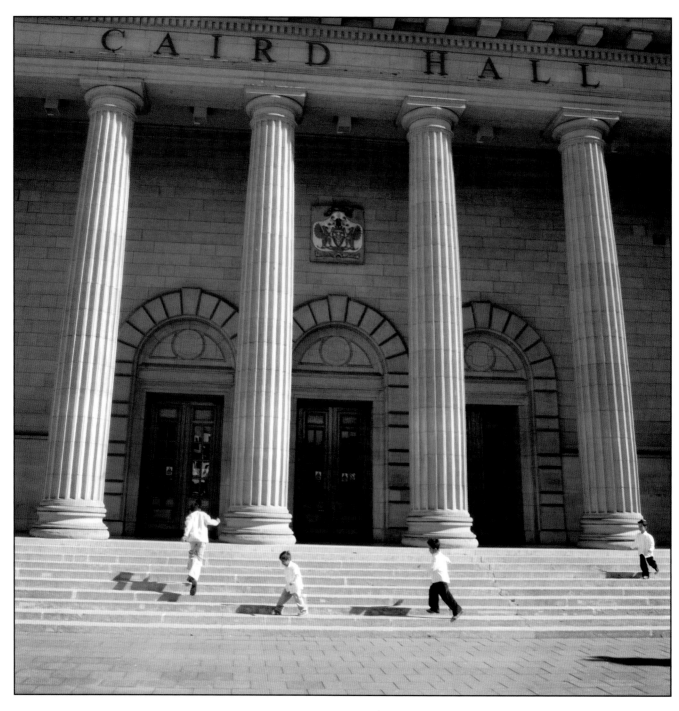

Are the boys playing truant, or running into a concert in the Caird Hall?

An exuberant performance of *Carmen* in the Caird Hall.

Susan Passfield on the steps of the Caird Hall, one of a team who bring class acts to this essential Dundee venue.

Second in the British Primary Skating Championships, Laura Kean is destined for even greater achievements.

The leaf of a banana Musa plant in the University of Dundee Botanic Garden.

Falling water in the miniature rock garden created by Jim Sutherland of Ardfearn Nursery, Inverness, soothes visitors to Dundee Flower and Food Festival in Camperdown Park, an annual event that attracts thousands over the two-day horticultural and culinary feast.

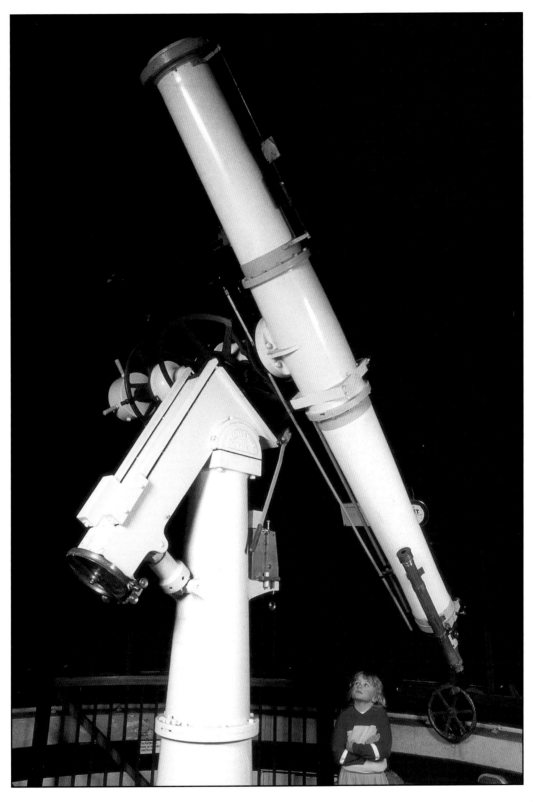

The child is star-struck at the 10 inch refracting telescope in the Mills Observatory, built by the devout John Mills, the linen and twine manufacturer, so that his fellow Dundonians could lift their eyes to the skies and wonder at divine creation as well as being educated in astronomy. The Mills Observatory is the only full-time observatory in the United Kingdom.

Dudhope Park's sylvan peace, a haven for
Dundonians and visitors

The Rep

Dundee's theatres were forced to take final curtain calls in the 1930s as audiences went to the cinema instead. However, Robert Thornely, the manager of the last touring company to perform in Dundee, was determined that his professional theatre company was not going to load its props on a lorry and depart the city. Thornely approached the Dundee Dramatic Society, an amateur company, which, also faced with nowhere to perform, had recently purchased its own premises in the form of a disused jute mill. In May 1939 professional and amateur thespians came together in the Dundee Repertory Theatre.

Dundonians needed drama and comedy to keep their minds off the possibility of an air raid. In the summer of 1963 fire succeeded where the Luftwaffe had failed, and the nomadic theatre company left the gutted mill to find refuge in a converted church in Lochee Road. For eighteen frustrating years it improvised as best it could, until Dundee District Council and the Scottish Arts Council agreed that the company would have its own purpose-built premises on land donated by the University of Dundee.

Bulldozers broke the frosty ground in 1979, but it looked as if the machines would have to be switched off due to rising costs and inflation. But Dundee had been through this drama before, and a public appeal raised £60,000 in under six weeks, reaching an eventual total of £200,000 in a city where money was scarce.

The new theatre opened on 8 April 1982. The 450 seater auditorium provided one of the best examples in Scotland of an audience close to the stage. The building received a civic commendation from The Civic Trust Award in 1984 and in 1986 won the RIBA Architecture Award.

Hamish Glen took centre stage in 1992. His artistic judgement and direction turned Dundee Rep into a long-running critical and commercial success. In 1996 it received the prestigious TMA Martini Award for the Best Overall Production in the UK and in September 1999 it opened its doors to one of the most ambitious experiments in Scottish Theatre for many years – a permanent company of 14 actors. Also at this time the Rep was undertaking major refurbishment and upgrading of its award-winning building, ensuring Dundee a state-of-the-art theatre in the city's new cultural quarter.

In the spring of 2003 with the departure of Hamish Glen, James Brining and Dominic Hill became joint Artistic Directors. They have taken the Rep's productions elsewhere in Scotland and further afield. It is said that a theatre's reputation and prosperity rest with the critics. They have been voting with their feet, for in the 2004 Critics Awards For Theatre In Scotland (CATS), Dundee Rep won five awards.

A warm invitation to
Dundee Rep's building
designed by the
Nicoll Russell Studio.

Samantha Young played Mrs Robinson's daughter Elaine in Dundee Rep's production of *The Graduate*.

Gypsy came to the Rep in the appealing form of Emily Winter.

The express arrives in the Rep, generating steam and energy as David Barrett plays Yonkers, and Richard Roe plays Tulsa in *Gypsy*.

More colourful action in *Gypsy*.

In Scottish Dance Theatre's £1 million plus dance studio at Dundee Rep Toby Fitzgibbons and Holly Warren perform in a piece called 404 by Austrian choreographer Willi Dorner. The Theatre is touring constantly, bringing the delights of dance to a wide audience.

Broughty Ferry

On a summer afternoon in Dundee East station the merchant prince in his wing collar sits in the carriage, watching the young ones in their blue sailor suits coming on with long-skirted mothers and nannies. They are all bound for Broughty Ferry, the merchant prince to his splendid house built on jute on the hill, the young ones to the beach. Now isn't it a pity that these urchins on the platform can't come because, he thinks, they look in need of a good wash?

But they don't have the sixpence for the bathers' return ticket because their mothers, who work in the merchant prince's mill, can't spare it. (The merchant prince will go home to a hot bath run by a servant). But don't be too hard on the gentleman in the wing collar: he does use some of his profits for public good. The merchant prince frowns and takes his watch from his waistcoat. But they're all aboard and the whistle goes, the steam train hurrying them along the shore of the estuary.

Before the railway arrived in 1838 Broughty Ferry was a cluster of fisherfolks' cottages round the harbour of Partan Craig (crab rock), and a square keep. This was 'the Brighton of Scotland,' and the trains kept steaming in all summer. The bathing-belles in their knee-long costumes have disappeared forever into the swell, but the occasional bikini can still be seen, climate permitting.

Don't think that the place has lost its summer zest, however. It's many years since the White Coons sang their swansong on the stand on the beach, but there's still plenty of entertainment. Broughty Ferry Traders, an association of more than 90 businesses, continue the tradition of a Gala Week in July, with attractions for all ages. In the old days there were donkey races; now there's Fun in the Park.

Now here's a mystery story. Night after night half a century ago folk noticed a light at the first floor window of a large house called Winsterly, where a man was bent over a leather-topped desk. The big Bible on a stand on the desk had notes in the margins, but that wasn't what he was working on, though he was a devout supporter of the Church of Christ in Dundee. Dudley D. Watkins was inspired, which was why he was working late. The name means nothing to you? Well, he is said to be the greatest comic artist that Britain has ever produced, and in that Broughty Ferry room night after night he drew Desperate Dan, Lord Snooty, Biffo the Bear, and others, which is why, some say, Desperate Dan is a Broughty man.

In 1838 the Dundee and Arbroath Railway opened, and the age of the commuter commenced by the Tay estuary.

Broughty Castle commands the Tay. The site might have been first fortified in 1454 when the Fourth Earl of Angus received permission to build there. It then changed hands many times before the second Lord Grey took ownership, and built the tower house that still forms the core of the castle. Broughty Castle was occupied by the English in 1550, and recovered, until taken by the Protestant Scots faction.

Bought by the Edinburgh and Northern Railway in 1846, the castle was restored by the famous Scottish architect R. Rowand Anderson for the War Office in 1861 as an outpost to control the Tay. The castle is now owned by Historic Scotland, but is staffed and run by Dundee City Council as a museum, housing fascinating displays on the life and times of Broughty Ferry, its people, the local environment and wildlife.

Broughty Castle's guns are purely ornamental.

'Thieves will need knock ere they enter' was the confident prediction of John Strachan when he erected Claypotts, a Z-plan towerhouse with gunholes on either side of the entrance, in the turbulent years of 1569-88. An Ancient Monument open to the public, Claypotts Castle is reputed to be haunted by a 'White Lady' who is seen at a window in the castle each 29 May. She is said to be the ghost of Marion Ogilvie, mistress of Cardinal Beaton, who was murdered at St Andrews on 29 May 1546. It seems churlish to spoil this story by pointing out that Claypotts had not been built by 1546, and that Marion lived at Melglund Castle.

This is no optical joke on the Broughty Ferry – Monifieth road at Reres Hill. Go round to the back of the big arch to get the gist: 'This gateway and fountain were erected in commemoration of Her Majesty's Jubilee by James Guthrie Orchar Esq Chief Magistrate of Broughty Ferry and were presented by him to the community on 19th September 1887.'

The gatehouse of Carbet Castle, 7 Camphill Road, Broughty Ferry, the residence of one of the most famous of Dundee's textile families, from whom the late Jo Grimond the Liberal leader was descended. The rivalry between the Grimonds and Gilroys led to the former trying to outdo their business rivals in the opulence of their residences. Both Carbet Castle and Castleroy were demolished because of dry rot, but the 1871 painted ceiling by Charles Frechou was saved from Carbet in an ingenious 'sandwich' operation and is in storage.

The oldest iron bridge in Scotland and one of the oldest in the world, Linlathen East footbridge spans the Dighty Burn at the eastern entrance to the grounds of Linlathen House, Broughty Ferry. Dating from 1795 to 1810, the bridge is now virtually unusable. However, the state of this bridge and others over the Dighty will be considered in a survey by Dundee City Council into access, environmental education and habitat enhancement.

The Seven Arches viaduct below Panmure Bleachfield carried the traffic of the Dundee and Forfar Direct Railway which was opened in 1870 by the Caledonian Railway Company for more direct communication between Dundee and Forfar. The line branched from the Dundee and Arbroath line at Broughty junction and had stations at Barnhill and Kingennie.

A Lifeboat has been stationed at Broughty Ferry since 1830, ready to launch in all weathers to save the crews of ships in distress among the treacherous sandbanks at the mouth of the Tay or much further out to sea. Broughty Ferry Lifeboat Station was rededicated on its 175th anniversary in the summer of 2005. The men and women who volunteer to crew the station's two Lifeboats are selfless in their endeavours for those in peril on the sea.

The blooms of Broughty Ferry.

Eastern Primary School, Broughty Ferry.

Are these three absorbed pupils at Forthill Primary School, Broughty Ferry, planning an expedition to the North Pole when they are older?

Self-portrait, Grove Academy, Broughty Ferry.

Wintry Beauty

Even in winter earth is lovely still,

Bared almost to the bone:

The clean anatomy of tree and hill;

The honesty of stone:

In ultimate endurance under the touch

Of fingering wind and frost:

Withered into a beauty beyond smutch

When all but all is lost:

An incorruptible and patient grace

From bravery forsworn:

The steadfastness upon an aged face

Out of long sufferance born.

William Soutar (1898-1943)

It is just as well that this slippery ascent to the McManus Galleries and Museum is no longer in use by the public.

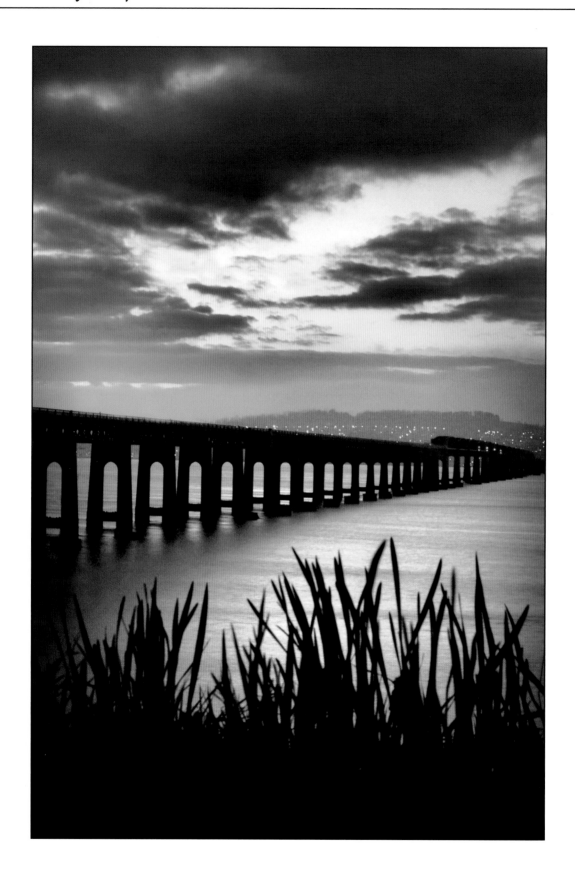

Looking across to Dundee from Newport-on-Tay.

The winter view towards Newport-on-Tay from the Tay road bridge.

A reminder that Dundee plays a major part in the oil industry.

Surrounded by the village of Ferryport-on-Craig, the white tower of Tayport Lighthouse is 58.8 feet tall. Its night character of white, red and green every three seconds has a range of 23 nautical miles.

O setting sun, as in thy red rays

Thou dost sink to night.

William Shakespeare (1564-1616)